DATA SHADOW

Dear Neil,

Best wishes,

Tony

DATA SHADOW

Tony Lopez

REALITY STREET EDITIONS
2000

Published by
REALITY STREET EDITIONS
4 Howard Court, Peckham Rye, London SE15 3PH

Acknowledgements and thanks to the Harold Hyam Wingate Foundation for a Wingate Scholarship awarded in 1996/97 which enabled the composition of this work; also to Nate Dorward, Andrew Duncan, Ross Leckie, Anthony Mellors, Ian Robinson, Simon Smith and John Tranter, who have published poems from this book in *Angel Exhaust, The Fiddlehead, Fragmente, The Gig, Jacket* and *Oasis.* An earlier version of "A Preface" was written for the 1998 Talks series curated by Bob Perelman at King's College, University of London. *Data Shadow* extends, completes and supplements the project begun with *False Memory* (The Figures, 1996), published thanks to Geoffrey Young.

Typesetting & book design by Ken Edwards
Front cover image by Tony Lopez

Eastern Arts Board Funded

Reality Street Editions is grateful to the Eastern Arts Board for making this book possible, in part, by providing funding

Printed & bound in Great Britain
by Doveton Press Ltd, Bristol

A catalogue record for this book is available from the British Library

ISBN: 1-874400-17-2

Contents

A Preface

When someone allows music to play upon them and to pour into the soul, all their experiences are muted out, and so is delayed the return of essentialist thinking. Language is rich in expressions of this cognitive mode, so internalised as to release the political from the tyranny of the self-evident. Should we not therefore will this state of culture beyond our natures into being? Those sweet and melancholy airs hydrate and gently smooth away all resistance, not to the absence, but to the contest of meanings in historical time. Each person will therefore be for themselves a person in the process of becoming, and beyond mere identity politics. It's a nice idea, but how do we get there, and what kind of salad are we building here? A sentence can be for life itself, or subject to parole: we forget so much. Why should we remember anything at all? Who has not said "it's on the tip of my tongue," meaning to attribute which particular function where? A shape known since it was squeezed out between the tongue and palate, first food or word. I like my tuna cooked just through; so is memory tasted and pronounced, the form is physical. For have I not shown in what follows that no intellectual good can come without involuntary pleasure?

Cultivated for its own development, poetry is not to be sacrificed to the labour of the community; for poetry, like sexual desire, has its own labour to accomplish. Incompleteness, perdurance, the refusal to make things fit, drives all our rhetoric towards a mistrust of philosophical resolutions and narrative false-consciousness. Do not unpack the spectre until you plan to use it, for the spectre haunts the merely empirical and is the meaning of unhappiness itself. The amazons of Libya had house-husbands to whom they returned after military service. They had deployed the hottest power pigment and wiped from their lips every trace of colour with ultrashine. Why should girls suddenly lose all confidence and hope at the age of twelve? Why do unabashed boys now follow them on lonely journeys into those far countries of anorexia and bulimia? Why have we accepted a radical increase in male suicide, addiction and educational failure? Count down to blast off and float away.

Very often no inferential path is available, introducing love between us as some story we could live or tell, accumulating family capital. Could we not imagine a family as an inclusive centre? For is not love the sign of determinate oscillation which is more than heaven allows? Only when it escapes the obscurity of the natural, and enters the virtual world of language, knowing breath as mediation. Now we see how rights construct each particular subject and each subjectivity, inscribing the possible into laws we must fight for. Many by the pipeline are made homeless and impoverished, and folds in this turbulent flow give us recursive symmetries from nonlinear functions. If we hold no converse with the Muses, does not even that intelligence which may be in us, grow disordered, dull and blind? Two arts are they, music and poetry, answering to each other in self-similarity, and only indirectly to the soul and body, in order that they may be relaxed or drawn tighter into due harmony.

The beginning season was late winter, which to a Londoner who has migrated south and west, is also the beginning of spring. The song-thrush (population reduced by forty percent in twenty years) sings upon the suburban rooftop at the passing of an early-morning satellite, stranger and more beautiful than our moon. Such thoughts as these might be implanted and carefully contextualised in a tiny virtual space such as a poem. Helicopters quarter the sky overhead, their heat-imaging cameras sweeping over the ground. Who are the fugitives? Virgil alone relates the story of Camilla strapped to her father's spear and thrown to safety on the far bank of the Armisenus river; her life was dedicated to Diana. It is as if the poet had, with a car-mechanic's intuition, started the motor that drives us still. As if he had foreseen Hegel's approach to love as the labour of opposites, contained within the fable of an infant warrior girl, flying on a spear.

Writers are building from negativity their overdetermined structures of contradictory desire. Yet the reasons are utterly ludicrous which they give in confirmation of their own notions of beauty and repose. A system inconsistent with respect to negation admits both a proposition and its opposite, being thus promiscuous and entering a high-risk infective group. And so is Philosophy left desolate, with her marriage rite incomplete, and these multinational conjunctions are likewise folded in. For meaning is a kind of music which can itself be ranged through shapes that develop in time. There is a seldom-mentioned prosody of meaning, folded into music, and projected beyond the person and the personal: really anywhere you want shimmer. Since it is possible to generalise this situation, it must be accepted that all formal systems have internal limitations, including logic and all languages that can be translated into it. Let's improvise a negation of negation in four-four time. Add "eg" to "nation" and preserve the rhyme. The invention of beauty was never a more urgent necessity and it may be our only hope of survival. I look forward to hearing from you, and meanwhile trust that the preparations for our symposium are going well.

Imitation of Life

If you are zinc deficient what you lose first
Is your sense of smell. Three human cases
Were chaotic rather than truly random
Due to tree-felling on the line. Ride into space
To wait an uncertain time in units called
Wave numbers. Disease erodes this memory.
I have seen Romanian shepherds piping
On TV, donnish yet funky prophets
Of deformed unshielded crystal. Too late
To convert speech into data packets,
Missing you already. Welcome to Heathrow's
Gate 31 automatic shopping mall.
Poles fall over and rot, why not leave them?
Chocolate and crisps to eat now or during your flight.

Two packs of melatonin,15% off,
Because I'm worth it. The perfect start to a day.
He has allowed the substance known as poetry
To be infected with agents that inhibit
Pain receptors. The tongue touches an electrode
But we cannot yet in a ruinous place
Be confident. Here comes the science bit:
Narrower towards the front teeth, a main verb.
The same intrinsic brightness cannot be sustained
After the closing date. Happy perpetual flow
Of trivial objects, melted and reduced.
Long term unpredictability is a good sign.
Now they begin to sense their physicality
Most owners want their satellites out of this region.

This application form should be accompanied
By voice-mail and personal calls. Fair Athena,
It's easier if we don't see one another
And fold back separate pages. Each syllable
Proved difficult to unravel. These exist
For first and second persons only, and agree
Like adjectives. A moment white then melts forever:
It's your natural charisma that should shine through
Not your face. We did not pull down the city
Nor the city walls, for the goddess saved us.
Forget lip gloss, discover our new creation
Without expensive research. I had in my hand
A small engraving of orbital space junk,
Caviar blinis, a cigar owned by Churchill.

Trade in seahorses makes speech melt away
Like metallic paint, face down in the snow.
Volunteer stewards are needed. Beat to beat
fluctuations from healthy hearts. Permanent black
In the path of electron tunnelling. Who knows?
Low maintenance, the ultimate beauty
Principle. A dead region of tissue
Sits on six hydraulic legs in all-day colour
More radiant with every use. You need tangibles.
You need new sources of sustained revenue
Even if you're red-shy. When a white dwarf
Swallows gas, time increases from left to right:
Patch it into any existing submarine cable
With a live video feed. A slow business.

City vending invites you to refresh yourself
With a fresh-brewed 3D simulator package
That clamps over the shoulder. By knowing size
And age at maturity, you can do hand-held:
You can split chaos from pure noise or fold it back in.
Target species caught at sea by hand or in nets,
Lost to medicine forever. A new shipment
Requires its own newsletter to be set up
In woven nomadic colours. No longer feeds.
Soon we could all be eating it. Knowledge hunger
A sudden decline in muscle cells. Wet data
Always begins with some injury or need.
Narrative formats persist in our wet brains,
Extraterrestrial garbage. No longer breeds.

I looked up and saw big jet trails crossed in the sky
Evening light, smoke blowing across the stadium:
They told me, Heracleitus, you were dead.
I heard the attenuation of sound
Moving through the sample, this can also be
Retrofitted. They brought me bitter news to hear
And bitter tears to shed. The origin
Of this complexity has long been forgotten.
The article is not used with the predicate
And there is a new national mainline map.
This latest edition details more services.
The English words are not exactly as given
In the vocabulary; think of synonyms.
They are chasing sailors into the market-place.

To the human eye, which cannot detect UV
That mental country is expected to decline
When compared with our thematic growth package.
War was unknown. Consumer groups approved
The packaged products and services of
Arethusa, who is the source of this sample.
The world is turning into information,
Store in an upright position. London ivy
The natural and delicious alternative
Sits awkwardly on screen. Asian tigers
Fail to bounce back for the demise of inflation.
Trainer and jockey in the best of form
Who wander into the Arcadian sunlight
Found in direct speech. One trillion bits per second.

Nothing works like repression in fixed circuits
To carry signals to the heart. Enjoys music,
Gardening, cinema, seeks funny male
Who must be genuine. Unlimited access,
Staggered vesting facilities, spin resonance
Left on the verge. The next crash in Tom-all-Alone's
May perpetuate the notion of brevity
But not always in pentameter. A final
Brief chapter. No mention of another fix.
We're launching plain vanilla funds no longer
Relax and feel the benefit. Well strung-out,
A stream which flowed underground for many years
Revealing the personality. No pine trees
Were felled to make keels. No walls surrounded cities.

It’s the most selfish act. Struck by a laser beam
The second and fourth lines of each stanza
Opt for income drawdown. A verbatim replay
Emerged in Syracuse but fails to reach
The rest of the body. Don’t underestimate
Your gut feeling. More radiant with every use,
The backward glance, the fragile equilibrium.
Are you sleep deficient? We seek no discount
But actual acquaintances of the poet
In waves of electrical excitation.
Knowledge of transgenic breeding is useful
As non-humans are not able to do this
For themselves. He draws on his aerospace background
For the reality of mud and trailer camps.

If the wave breaks apart, strict repetition
Saves exhausted and contaminated paper
On the Etruscan ridges. They never knew
What they were working on. It was simple
Competing for space on oestrogen receptors:
Silicon is the normal base. We'll call her
Princess DNA. The actual words
Reappear in the previous paragraph.
Hundreds of captives transported to Persia.
A man around whom complications gather
At the end of a long bull market. Camilla
Was a Volscian nursed by a wild mare
And with her shaft of pine she ran him through.
Tiny rings of DNA are killing us all.

Restricted Zone (slight return)

How could the mind take hold of such a country
In which white heaps build up and ivy covers
The early industrial era? Chimneys seem
To contain many things long and short. No smoke
From these abandoned engines. Wires converge
On a ring attached to a wooden pole
With ceramic fittings. “Someone’s with me in RL,”
It said, “Ask Janine about her new ID.”
Plastic moulded into bone-shaped buttons.
A small noun, head down in a damp field,
Cropping verbs uncovered in the present
Continuous. Beyond the bullet-proof glass
He smiles and waves — our man in developing states —
Coming down on liberation theology.

Luminous rape under grey cloud shows red
In the satellite heat picture. We're proud of our people.
A yellow shirt on platform five explodes the subject,
Testing visual and orthographic processing.
Policies based on instruments such as green-belt
Have little effect on the shape of metropolis.
Every neighbourhood in parameter space
Finds the nearest periodic attractor. Innovation,
Technical know-how, attention to detail —
Casting the French-polisher from *Yellow Pages*
For his trusty face. A sleep-out on Mt Igman
With a minimum four hundred knots to the inch.
Snow holes, barbecue, good definition
In fractal clusters grown using local rules.

5AM on the tree-lined campus
As scholars arrive in the back seats of taxis
Met from the sleeper train, still a bit sleepy,
Radiators, shelves, glass — things just falling.
We ran to the toilets for cover, hoping
For a little shut-eye ahead of registration
If the porter would open up a study-bedroom.
Just an accident of where you live and how
You hold a pencil, listening for metal wheels
Hitting joints in the rails, car horns each to each.
Streets are familiar but not quite right,
A fine blue morning with high cloud.
The rabbits up early, out on the lawns
Ready to feed and have their photos taken.

This is the beginning of a poetry conference.
Linen trousers are supposed to look as if
You slept in them. Windows sucked out of buildings
A quarter of a mile away. We took it
Back to focus group 21, weighed down
With items for the delegates' book table;
Whether relaxing, doing odd jobs round the house,
Or out and about in the car. Still sleepy
On *Glenfiddich* and *Temazepan.*
Getting rid of a pocket full of pound coins
Is a good idea, in the centre of Manchester
Or any city. Your open container
Drips onto plastic mulch. Red flow from a car boot:
All you do is listen and the stories come to life.

In multitudinous chatterings, she sees through
Simulation to the bone — pity and fear
Is what we feel, working through outmoded systems:
What else can a mother give her daughter?
A beautiful riff in time, say March in 44 BC.
Lost incomprehensible affect, lost feelings,
Truth lies hidden in a deep unfashionable well.
Years when Italy was torn. Therefore I resign
All claim to this experience, reading,
Writing, sailing a boat, getting hit on the head
In not-quite unison. Uffington white horse
Cut in the iron age. Photo by *Aerofilms.*
But since ferns have no seed, where would you cast them,
Knowing that each single angel is terrible?

The coiled wires are red, yellow and green
Running from the cab. Let's set up a phone-in.
Biting through leaves, tarpaulin, and good rope
To arrive at Brodmann's areas 44/45.
An infectious protein that attacks the brain
Known as a prion. Surviving heat treatment,
We are still hoping to make our connection
Following a white line and red lights ahead.
A complex pattern of frequency-locking
Is better than no pattern at all. *Air Ride Suspension.*
Systems with many degrees of freedom
Such as turbulent fluids, fibrillating hearts,
Movements of populations in real cities:
This medium makes gender surfing possible.

This is how we stabilise a chaotic array
In neurologically normal right-handed males:
From permutation to negativity
A simple but non-trivial pattern emerges
Which cannot be called unconscious.
Breathing in small particles of you, which
Already have their receptors, so that
When you raise an arm to push back your hair
And shift slightly in your seat, aware or not,
The faintest trace upon the air invents
This utterance. She would pronounce "semiotic"
Licking the moisture off and causing more
To arrive. The number of pixels showing
Activation in the inferior frontal gyrus.

I recollect the council was going green
And we announced it right after the phone-in
On the Auschwitz bus-trip. Give them more rope
And play-back time. Being born before '45
Was a basic qualification. No brain-
Dead Surrealists, no special treatment:
Neo-modernists break their own connections
Or drop off the classics list. We will stay ahead
Only by vocabulary-locking.
The future is bright, with temporal suspension,
Wir machen den weg frei: customer freedom
Is the feeling we hope for in all our hearts.
Country weekends, trouble free return to city
Apartments: let us make your dream possible.

Thus troubled clergy in the northern diocese
Learnt the boundaries of clerical morality.
"Dual containment" looks increasingly futile
To a palsied youth locked into a war game
Scenario. His car crashed, clothes ablaze,
Who did not close his eyes for seven days
But continued to steer and use the foot-pedals,
Cutting out some heavy-handed melodrama,
Which floats in a pool of light on Dundee's stage.
Universals appear to run through the system.
Bombing speaks to no-one but pushes up prices
And frightens the children. We brought them back
With careful friendly speech, then hypnotherapy,
In a corner flat in building 132.

You can lock up kids but it doesn't change
Behaviour patterns. Here comes the Euro:
Plenty of soft edges, moving to Dagenham.
The ward was filled with amputee children
Meeting the deficit target. Worries about
The peaceful integration of disparate states
Are irrational. Genetic engineering
Helps to make sure the output gap is clawed back:
The safety of your corn plant is unfounded.
Now that self-assessment is approaching
You need to put some instruments in place: invest.
We don't shoot the messenger. Now find the umbrella:
A target for Serbian shells. This guarantee
Does not affect your statutory rights.

Speckled Noise

Give me intimate and penetrating studies
Of human behaviour, engineered leak-proof
In a thick but appropriate magenta.
It's hard to imagine an easier or more
Intuitive system. Their jewelled ear-rings
Screwed tight into unpierced ears, depend upon
The very language of the fish market
Which deters the meanest rash action. It was
No ordinary Monday bought in ready-made
Since we cut back on location dramas.
Well sourced or not, it's all interpretation:
Whether you play the standards to old tunes,
Or in a sudden frenzied modernity, seek to
Become the grunge idol of a million slackers.

We would promenade, when some curious passer-by
(In feathers raped from the osprey) was heard to say,
"How do birds smell red or hear green?" Let me tell you
It was no such uncommon thing to be blinded
By the extreme vividness of their exterior;
Some startling and quite pointless convolution of
Blue muslin, yellow hair and high quality drama.
No-one wants to be a teenager anymore.
These holographic images are heat-stable
But readily erased by circularly
Polarised light. Now conceive you a great passion
And loftiness of manner in this lamentably
Absurd lapse from verity. So: wheezing, sneezing,
Came in the small men with black and rosy faces.

I travelled with that worthy gentleman
Who brought over a patent under the broad seal
For our governance. Addicted to late dinner
He employed a sabbatical vocalist
To sing only anthems and oratorios
And inaugurate the winter season. So I
Experienced the higher than ambient flux
In equatorial pacific. I found me
Isotopic traces of export production:
Continental dust preserved in ice cores
Of Greenland and Antarctica. Such a muffled
And musty smell came from his adopted frock-coats
Beneath gothic canopies of fumed oak
In our artistic and half-timbered cafes.

You may wonder why our ready-gel is causing
So much excitement, since there is more news
Than a paper has room to print. Impossible
Assertions occlude the real purpose of the work
Which leaked out of the banking system. Normally
A liquidator is appointed but buyers
Get no compensation. Simply collect 8 tokens
And join the queue for post-war restitution
(Don't even ask about the price of dental work).
Lawyers, notaries and fiduciaries have all
Just been lonely too long. Not a nail on the wall —
No chair, no table, no straw mattress, nothing.
But they did not concede that this was the amount
Held back with vast sums of production money.

These then were the lessons of American
Narrative process, script driven, whose unspoken
Allegation of transcendentalised high tea
Faded like an old sugared biscuit in a
Second-empire scheme of chocolate, turquoise-
Blue and gold. Benefits include personal calls
Office sex, internet access — it's a sad day
For investigative journalism. She/he sang
"I want to be a cowboy's sweetheart, for they
Are so expressive in their dress and adornments."
Our strongest impression was a kindly
Timidity: tinkle, trill and sweetly jingle,
Silly as any alpine cowbell you may hear
In one of those old-time menthol tobacco ads.

The review is broken into two parts
Each of which begins with an oversized drop-cap
To introduce this fairy tale of nothingness.
They put to sea with a prosperous wind, and now
Being compact together in one ship, declare
It is not enough to call for northern sunlight
We must demonstrate our serious commitment
To support, deliver and reward these ladies
Of fabulous age, celebrity scholars and
Post-modern architects. Language such as "soothe"
"Calm" and "reasoned" reinforces this tendency
More steadily as the election approaches.
A dramatic increase in phytoplankton growth
Turns the sea at last from blue to green.

And this fine emancipatory thought was come
On my afternoon walk, so that at once I saw
The promenade with its south-facing windows.
Sister Midnight, who looked severely at the band
Sporting a corraline stethoscope, told us
Her house had become "a perfect museum." She was
Trading off-plan conversions of inner-city
Old industrial buildings, getting in the way
Of small random errors in voting intentions.
Total DNA blots, prepared with DNA
From human tumour, foetal and normal tissue,
Are pre-tested to ensure the presence of
Full-length transcripts. We will where possible avoid
The expense of pursuing judicial reviews.

A gentle push of cam closures fastens the gate
And guides cattle to the crusher for de-horning
Without undue pain. We have outstanding
Image brightness, motorised photo-functions,
Absolute data security. How about
This millennial project? A virtual building —
No gravity or planning disputes, open to all.
No-one has been murdered on London's underground
As yet. Editing numbers appear on each frame.
In the world of viruses, we are invaders.
This skylight speech is no accidental figure
taken up for eloquence and now abandoned
In some dumb remake of *Clueless.* You're stuck inside
The engine room of the knowledge society.

We crawled on bubble plastic in the roof space
(A new performance, this) so that try as we may
There was quite a racket in the engine room.
But we needed an experienced oracle
Developer, designer or analyst
To set up the cash cow, extended warranties,
Little beads drifting in magnetised fluid.
Gradually this uncertain chronology
Hardened into historical record, so that
We were stuck with sclerotic it. A group tour
In front of an 11 foot screen, steering
With a joystick. We could follow the adventures of
Mary Kingsley who, armed with an umbrella,
Foraged among mangrove swamps seeking specimens.

When through blue lips they murmured that a paper
May well switch allegiance, it was news to some
Apparently. Best chill the rice before you stir-fry
Drifting gradually eastwards. How was it
That such a fortunate concatenation
Of circumstances came to be? Why not eat speech?
A method of seismic energy transfer,
You mix it up with vegetables and red ink.
Go on: popular culture binds us together
If anything does. Gerunds like Gladstone bags
Remind us of long dead politicians who
Develop through controlled underground explosions
Or outmoded travel accessories. Meaning
Is something we lost back in 1973.

Always Read the Label

This body does not contain an index, but is
Otherwise spontaneous, unrestrained, natural —
Made from the finest time-dated TV footage:
Ironic, absurd, full of self mockery. Shot
In one of those rambling clapboard houses
Like a brilliant parody of criticism
Which says nothing at all. Shut the jewel case.
Belief in God may not be sufficient protection
For the under-capitalised, so that
The following year you'll be back where you started
In a blood-spattered cowshed. You can leave early
(Weather permitting) float into a delirium.
"Shut the jewel case like a good boy" she said,
"History just doesn't happen everywhere."

You begin not by picking up the powerbook
But by deciding to begin. Here we are
Established in a freezing pinch of the feet.
The smoke bush is another example.
Inuit are at the top of their food chain
In the ultimate chemical dump. Boil water,
Cook your meat right through, demand a second ballot.
You can't get a solution by proxy
In any aspect but the purely visual.
These are real flaws in the non-profit ethic
To which is subjoined the machinery of this
My eclogue, old and well publicised in the night sky.
The entire braid can be coded as a sequence
And thus receive your troubled delegation.

Patrick was the name of the day as I heard it —
Slide into the seat, put your hands at the wheel
And feel our glorious Teutonic past. No bugs.
A fabulously elliptical house style.
Governments control this data. There will be no
Opportunity for lunch. Small business users
Are welcome on the field trip to St Elizabeth's
With chill-out rooms for true skaters. Our psychodrama
In a strange labyrinthine palace of ice.
It means something like "deep home" but with overtones
Of hatred and loathing. Things and persons always
Already alien. The worst fears of researchers:
Forests haunted by shapeless apparitions
From the middle-England mail-order catalogue.

Why is it that a man seems so sinister
Wearing gloves indoors? Someone says “mind the gap”
As he moves along measuring table settings.
These are things and persons always already
Innocent in the soft verges. Don’t leave the lights on —
They will kill you for a shovelful of small coals.
Martha, the world’s last passenger pigeon, long dead.
Soft-feel fibres and drizzle-paint, pink on light brown.
This glass is wrapped for your personal use
It won’t last so call Stewart. Gold in your teeth.
A floor-proximity guidance system
Will direct you to the exit. Remain seated.
Call Anne today on a quiet cul-de-sac.
Double car port, cheaper than renting, call Eddy.

Unsteady on his legs in Omega cottage,
He bent down to pick up the lion. This set,
A translated grove with low maintenance
Corals and sponges, comes with deep-yellow flicker.
She wiped the points of her nail-scissors to retard
Clonal reproduction and complete the crossword.
A Canadian cadence to that voice. Red or green?
Slipping on wet marble slabs, we look up
At the LCD information panel. No trains.
Asda price, pocket the *différance.* Replace
The mindset. Up the broad avenue into town
Obviate the need for costly simulations.
The explicit limit of our instructions is
That the icon convey mean time to extinction.

Call it a “family” toothbrush, spin on about
Delicate gum tissue (bleeding round the teeth)
In the later bracketed line. Let’s go for
Rapid expansion out of Protestant theory:
Quality, Deep House and Trance. “More relaxed” still means
The perfect “more relaxed” outfit. You’ll need gloves
And a tank for surgical waste. Ishi, the last
Wild Indian of California, spent his
Days in the anthropological museum —
He just couldn’t cope with San Francisco.
You can phone researchers and tell them your story
In unannotated regions of *E. coli*
Chromosomes. Transcripts completely updated and
Tastefully landscaped. Buy now, choose your own colours.

From time to time we may pass on your name
To other, carefully selected companies
That ferry impulses above the brain stem.
No live model could stay in place night and day.
Please select another channel. Pull the mask
Towards you and breathe normally to download
A fully-functional demo version. At the epoch
Of last scattering, ordinary matter
Was dumped all over the Hubble sphere.
Now the dim gods of death have in their keeping
Mere protein fragments. You take out bone marrow
Add your viral vector, put the bone marrow back.
Palatino is fine — but I prefer Caslon.
It's a genuine pleasure having you on board.

Dummies sometimes take the place of real people
To see how badly they might have been hurt.
We encourage you to watch the video
Which is for your own welfare. Everything downstream
Of the blood clot was either politically
Unstable or subject to hormonal surges.
It was "extremely unlikely" that the canisters
Could have broken up in the atmosphere.
What if the Continuity Army Council
Neither consented nor refused to complete the trade?
If no Wimbledon train is shown, take the next
Dimmer switch that comes on gradually
In foetal development. Pressure of light
Produces gold-plated stars. When does pain begin?

The so-called nonsemantic features of language
Never had time to be beautiful. Hold fingers
Horizontally touching your forehead
To show the amount. Tongue and groove boarding
In a plausible context, one of the plots
Is newly dug. These are voluntary targets
A little nonplussed by your stoical charm
Having issued writs, free pens and mouse mats.
A strip of brain tissue that hugs the surface
Causing a massive increase in drag. Implants could
Translate prejudice directly into votes:
A whole panel of buttons that must be pushed.
Pain without cognition. No other network
Covers more of the UK population.

Britain, perfect for filming period drama
And convenient for *Eurodisney,* appears
To be rising more slowly. The prospect of ermine
Keeps eclipsed former ministers in order;
Reducing the appearance of wrinkles, which are
Broader and deeper than one might expect,
Marching into the second chamber. Hello John.
When the hounds of spring are on winter's traces
There may be no mortgage and no purchase
Despite low entry and exit costs. Most victims
Were homeless men sleeping rough but holding fast
To core principles. Sleet threatened, snow was alleged —
Broadcast on two cable networks. Making the dream
A reality, surrounded by spotty dogs.

Radial Symmetry

The reliquary of St Chad contained bones from
Three legs which, if not in actual ownership,
Comprised a new threat to passenger safety.
Guerrillas spent the early days of the siege
Watching TV for the first time. Here the weary
Traveller will find stress and memory loss
In abandoned and vandalised public parks.
List brokers selling shareholders' names. Such products
Appeared in most industrialised countries
And provided a notion of community
For branded global foods. 7000 vehicles
Under spotlights behind razor-wire fencing:
People firing bullets into the air. Soft drinks.
The confidential odour of enormous books.

Narrative must persist beyond such events
Or we should float unanchored and rudderless
In some unfathomable sea. Headless statues
Made over by an image consultant
From the consistory court. You'll find them both
In my Indian bag. About 70 genes
Have not been deleted so far: hundreds of men
Came out of the ground in foraging parties,
And hybrid fertility is very low.
I was enjoined to eat a good breakfast before
DNA-testing of the relics of saints
In a commercial plantation. A new, higher,
Homozygotic peak, like a wasp in a lyric
Whenever Hamilton's rule is satisfied.

It was a chill, blue-fingered hour and the gardens
Were nearly empty, as will often be true
In structured or viscous populations. After
Some agonising moments with hairpins, we
Attended to a paper on rapid changes
In the geological record. These "pages"
Were not pages at all but information dumps
Big as Bayreuth backdrops. Such variation
May be factored out to reveal a new reading
Of male relationships running through the book.
Stylish, slim M, played with immense authority
Seals his grip on the party. Pools of selected
Mutant genes produce a tremendous performance
Of baffled resentment: a cow for a few beans.

All these methods are seriously flawed.
Extinction probability is a product
Of fitness and speciation. Whether or not
Wrecked car parts stacked on rooftops constitutes
A planning violation, we should move away.
Disaster movies need terminal sequencing.
You may not reach adaptive optima
Or resist repeated invasion by clones.
The American civil war stopped the export
Of cotton. Are we a nation of shoplifters?
Stylish, fair, slim. Easygoing F, 36.
Male-biased dispersal, direct no-nonsense style.
"I want to live in the future," he says,
Painting eyes on a transparent screen.

This herring is a pretty fish. We are looking
At the degree of ornamentation beyond
Future survival prospects. An individual
Could be a sterile worker, isolated by
Distance and genetic redundancy, outwith
The rim of standard English. Post-segregational
Killing is not a unique function of surface
Exposure, but we have yet to run
A capital needs analysis. Little drops
Of lavender water, a minute handkerchief
Gritty with lace. Ancient conserved protein families.
Whatever leaks from the reference pile.
Many of these are careful and exquisite
Now that ashes serve to thicken his mixes.

The unofficial shortlist, taped to my windscreen,
Looked like a threat. Who cares what the magistrate says
For moral guidance? We advise selling old-style
Government offices. Open at thirty-six
Million. Come down heavy on shoplifters.
We could demerge tomorrow. The word "export"
Indicates higher alcohol level. These clones
Are fed to their lean bodyweight optima.
Bioremediation is about sequencing
Of nutrients: bacterial take-away
Hoovers up the oil spill. None of this constitutes
A written contract and the supplier will not
Be responsible for loss beyond product
Value. Why was our market intelligence flawed?

Who decided to air freight Egyptian beans?
How much can we lose? So-called high performance
Investment funds prey on carefully selected
Undervalued companies. No authority
Can protect border-crossing species. This new book
Will help you to overcome fear of reading
Aloud. Value criteria variations
As a method of corporate change. No-one dumps
In local rivers anymore. We have pages
Running next to features you'll love. Money changes
Hands. Discreetly filmed and interviewed, we
Loved to watch ourselves shopping. This was after
Double vouchers and cashback. Can it be true?
A year's free subscription to *Royal Gardens*?

Based at our vibrant and informal offices,
You would enjoy free permanent health insurance,
Money recycling, preferential share options.
Robin Hood has changed sides. Power lines above
Permanent way. Deep in the rain forest he finds
Polynesian families watching London news:
Cross-border Christmas shopping down 80 percent.
Evidence from tree-rings, pollen analysis,
And other paleoclimate records shows that
Normal healthy sperm production follows
The lunar cycle. Earth must have encountered
Dense clumps of dark matter in space. We have
Genome data from *Escherichia coli*
Served on a bed of seasonal leaf salad.

Some of these points, known as seismic gaps, are explained
As simple outcomes of random processes
Swallowing up identity. We ask them
To re-enact their purchases whilst we measure
Pupil dilation and subsequent aftershocks
In a region known as the outer rise. Butter
Trickles down his leg. Was Magwitch a paedophile?
Where are the wild export markets that used to be?
Most of these drugs are obsolete. Breakdown products
From a detergent used in the manufacture
Of paper, textiles and plastics. Oestrogens
Somehow leaking into the water supply.
With practice you'll wake up right inside the action
And experience the dream as real as your life.

A smooth laminar stream dissolved the surface.
Mist drifted over the pool of London. I woke
In the abstract sea of unspecified emotion.
Big tour operators are working to patch this
Through a headset. An uncle running up to bowl,
Someone sampling smut. Taste of lemons and oysters.
Music has downsized in tune with the casual look
Now transcending fashion as such. Radiation
And sudden exposure to market forces
Stripped out early consumer activity.
Should another mail arrive from Europe today
Be sure to be clear that we have completely
Conflicting visions of the future. Tick if you
Would prefer not to receive this material.

Also by Tony Lopez:

Snapshots
The English Disease
Change
Abstract & Delicious
A Handbook of British Birds
A Theory of Surplus Labour
Stress Management
Negative Equity
False Memory
Devolution

Other titles published by Reality Street Editions:

Nicole Brossard: *Typhon Dru*
Cris Cheek/Sianed Jones: *Songs From Navigation*
Kelvin Corcoran: *Lyric Lyric*
Ken Edwards: *Futures*
Allen Fisher: *Dispossession and Cure*
Susan Gevirtz: *Taken Place*
Barbara Guest: *If So, Tell Me*
Fanny Howe: *O'Clock* (O/P)
Sarah Kirsch: *T*
Maggie O'Sullivan: *In the House of the Shaman* (O/P)
Denise Riley: *Mop Mop Georgette* (O/P)
Peter Riley: *Distant Points* (O/P)
Lisa Robertson: *Debbie: an Epic*
Maurice Scully: *Steps*

Out of Everywhere: linguistically innovative poetry by women in North America & the UK (ed. by Maggie O'Sullivan)

RSE 4Packs
No. 1: *Sleight of Foot* (Miles Champion, Helen Kidd, Harriet Tarlo, Scott Thurston)
No. 2: *Vital Movement* (Andy Brown, Jennifer Chalmers, Mike Higgins, Ira Lightman)
No. 3: *New Tonal Language* (Patricia Farrell, Shelby Matthews, Simon Perril, Keston Sutherland)

Reality Street Editions depends for its continuing existence on grants from funding bodies, sales and subscriptions, and donations from the following Supporters:

Alfred David Editions
Dodie Bellamy/Kevin Killian
Karlien van den Beukel
Richard Caddel
John Cayley
Kelvin Corcoran
Michael Finnissy
Sarah Gall
Harry Gilonis/Elizabeth James
John Hall
Alan Halsey
Robert Hampson
Randolph Healy
Peter Hodgkiss
Fanny Howe
Romana Huk
Nicholas Johnson
L Kiew
Peter Larkin
Tony Lopez
The Many Press/John Welch
Peter Middleton
Drew Milne
Edwin Morgan
Douglas Oliver
Michael Palmer
Bob Perelman
Marjorie Perloff
Frances Presley
Ian Robinson
Will Rowe
Pete Smith
Spanner/Allen Fisher
Harriet Tarlo
Andrew Toovey
Keith Tuma
Marjorie Welish
5 x anonymous

For details of how to become a Reality Street Supporter, or to be put on the mailing list for news of forthcoming publications, write to the address on the reverse of the title page, or email **reality.street@virgin.net**

Visit our web site at: **http://freespace.virgin.net/reality.street**